# EASY AND QUICK KETOGENIC COOKBOOK

## FAST AND FLAVORFUL KETO DISHES

D1521502

## MARY M. VANISH

# ABOUT THE AUTHOR

**Mary M. Vanish** has dedicated her life to promoting healthy living through delicious and accessible cooking. A passionate advocate for nutritious eating, Mary has authored numerous cookbooks that focus on making wholesome meals achievable for everyone, regardless of their busy schedules.

Mary's journey into the culinary world began with her own quest for a healthier lifestyle. Through extensive research and experimentation, she discovered the transformative benefits of the ketogenic diet. This sparked her mission to share her knowledge and recipes with others, helping them to achieve their health goals without sacrificing flavor or enjoyment.

Married and a mother of two, Mary understands the challenges of balancing family life with maintaining a healthy diet. Her recipes are designed with simplicity and speed in mind, ensuring that even the busiest individuals can prepare and enjoy nutritious meals. Her family serves as both her inspiration and her enthusiastic taste-testers, ensuring that every dish in her cookbooks is family-approved.

In the **Easy and Quick Ketogenic Cookbook**, Mary combines her expertise in the keto lifestyle with her practical approach to cooking. Her goal is to make healthy eating accessible and enjoyable for everyone, providing recipes that are not only quick and easy but also delicious and satisfying.

Mary's commitment to healthy living extends beyond her cookbooks. She frequently conducts workshops and cooking classes, sharing her tips and techniques with a wider audience. Her approachable style and dedication to wellness have made her a beloved figure in the healthy cooking community.

Join Mary M. Vanish on a culinary journey that will transform the way you think about healthy eating. With her guidance, you'll discover that preparing nutritious and delicious keto meals can be both simple and rewarding.

# Table of Contents

# INTRODUCTION

## WELCOME TO THE EASY AND QUICK KETOGENIC COOKBOOK

Embarking on a ketogenic journey doesn't have to be complicated or time-consuming. In today's fast-paced world, many of us struggle to find the balance between maintaining a healthy lifestyle and managing our busy schedules. This cookbook is designed to bridge that gap, offering you a collection of delicious, nutritious, and easy-to-make recipes that align with the ketogenic lifestyle.

The ketogenic diet, commonly known as the keto diet, focuses on low-carb, high-fat foods that help your body enter a state of ketosis. In ketosis, your body becomes incredibly efficient at burning fat for energy. Beyond weight loss, the keto diet has been praised for improving mental clarity, boosting energy levels, and supporting overall health and well-being.

But let's face it: finding the time to cook healthy meals can be a challenge. That's why the **Easy and Quick Ketogenic Cookbook** is your perfect companion. Whether you're a seasoned keto enthusiast or just starting out, this cookbook provides a variety of recipes that can be prepared in 30 minutes or less, ensuring you spend less time in the kitchen and more time enjoying life.

**Inside, you'll find:**

- **Breakfast Delights:** Kickstart your day with energizing recipes that are both satisfying and quick to prepare.
- **Lunchtime Favorites:** Discover meals that are perfect for a quick lunch at home or to pack for work.
- **Dinner Solutions:** Enjoy hearty and fulfilling dinners that don't require hours of preparation.
- **Snacks and Appetizers:** Keep your cravings at bay with tasty and keto-friendly snacks.
- **Sweet Treats:** Indulge in desserts that are low in carbs but high in flavor.

Each recipe is crafted with simple ingredients and straightforward instructions, making keto cooking accessible to everyone, regardless of culinary skill level. You'll also find tips and tricks to maximize your time in the kitchen, ensuring that preparing keto meals becomes a stress-free and enjoyable part of your daily routine.

Join us on this culinary adventure as we explore the delicious possibilities of the keto diet. With the **Easy and Quick Ketogenic Cookbook**, you'll discover that eating healthy doesn't have to be a chore – it can be a delight.

Let's get cooking and start enjoying the benefits of the keto lifestyle today!

# CHAPTER 1
## BREAKFAST DELIGHTS:

## BACON AND EGG MUFFINS

**Serving Size**:6 muffins
Prep Time: 10 minutes
Cooking Time:20 minutes

**Nutrition Info (per serving):**
- Calories: 220
- Total Fat: 15g
- Saturated Fat: 6g
- Cholesterol: 220mg
- Sodium: 400mg
- Total Carbohydrates: 2g
- Protein: 18g

**Ingredients**:
- 6 slices of bacon
- 6 large eggs
- Salt and pepper to taste
- Optional: shredded cheese, diced vegetables like bell peppers or spinach

**Directions**:
1. Preheat your oven to 375°F (190°C). Grease a muffin tin with cooking spray or line with muffin liners.
2. In a skillet over medium heat, cook the bacon until it's crispy. Once cooked, remove the bacon from the skillet and let it cool on a paper towel-lined plate. Once cooled, chop the bacon into small pieces.
3. In a bowl, crack the eggs and whisk them together. Season with salt and pepper to taste.
4. If using, stir in any optional ingredients like shredded cheese or diced vegetables into the egg mixture.
5. Pour the egg mixture evenly into each muffin cup, filling them about halfway.
6. Sprinkle the chopped bacon evenly over the egg mixture in each muffin cup.
7. Place the muffin tin in the preheated oven and bake for 15-20 minutes, or until the egg muffins are set and slightly golden on top.
8. Once cooked, remove the muffin tin from the oven and let the muffins cool for a few minutes before removing them from the tin.
9. Serve the bacon and egg muffins warm, either on their own or with a side of toast or fresh fruit for a complete breakfast. Enjoy!

# KETO SAUSAGE AND CHEESE OMELETTE

**Serving Size**: 1 omelette
Cooking Time: 10 minutes
Prep Time: 5 minutes

**Nutrition Info (per serving):**
- Calories: 450
- Total Fat: 35g
- Total Carbohydrates: 2g
- Protein: 27g

**Ingredients:**
- 2 large eggs
- 2 ounces of breakfast sausage, cooked and crumbled
- 1/4 cup shredded cheddar cheese
- Salt and pepper to taste
- 1 tablespoon butter or oil for cooking

**Directions:**
1. In a bowl, beat the eggs until well mixed. Season with salt and pepper.
2. Heat butter or oil in a non-stick skillet over medium heat.
3. Pour the beaten eggs into the skillet and let them cook for about 1-2 minutes, until the edges start to set.
4. Sprinkle the cooked sausage evenly over the eggs.
5. Once the edges of the eggs are set, use a spatula to gently lift the edges and let the uncooked egg flow underneath.
6. Sprinkle shredded cheese evenly over the sausage.
7. Continue cooking until the eggs are fully set and the cheese is melted, about 2-3 minutes.
8. Carefully fold the omelette in half using the spatula.
9. Slide the omelette onto a plate and serve hot.

# ALMOND FLOUR WAFFLES

**Serving Size:** Makes about 4 waffles
Prep Time: 10 minutes

Cooking Time: 10 minutes

**Nutrition Info (per waffle):**
- Calories: 180
- Total Fat: 14g
- Saturated Fat: 2g
- Cholesterol: 50mg
- Sodium: 250mg
- Total Carbohydrates: 6g
- Dietary Fiber: 3g
- Sugars: 1g
- Protein: 8g

**Ingredients:**
- 1 1/2 cups almond flour
- 2 eggs
- 1/4 cup unsweetened almond milk
- 2 tablespoons melted coconut oil or butter
- 1 tablespoon sweetener of choice (such as honey or maple syrup)
- 1 teaspoon baking powder
- 1/2 teaspoon vanilla extract
- Pinch of salt

**Directions**:
1. Preheat Waffle Iron: Preheat your waffle iron according to manufacturer's instructions.
2. Mix Dry Ingredients: In a mixing bowl, combine almond flour, baking powder, and a pinch of salt. Stir until well combined.
3. Whisk Wet Ingredients: In another bowl, whisk together eggs, almond milk, melted coconut oil or butter, sweetener, and vanilla extract until smooth.

4. Combine Wet and Dry Ingredients: Pour the wet ingredients into the dry ingredients and stir until just combined. Be careful not to overmix.

5. Cook Waffles: Lightly grease the waffle iron with coconut oil or cooking spray. Pour enough batter onto the hot waffle iron to cover the grids, then close the lid and cook according to the manufacturer's instructions, usually about 3-5 minutes, or until golden brown and crisp.

6. Serve: Once cooked, carefully remove the waffles from the iron and serve warm with your favorite toppings such as fresh berries, sliced bananas, a drizzle of maple syrup, or a dollop of Greek yogurt.

7. Enjoy: Dig in and enjoy these delicious almond flour waffles guilt-free! They're perfect for a leisurely weekend breakfast or a quick weekday treat.

# SPINACH AND FETA BREAKFAST MUFFINS

**Serving Size**: 12 muffins
Prep Time: 15 minutes
Cooking Time: 25 minutes

**Nutrition Info (per muffin):**
- Calories: 150
- Total Fat: 9g
- Saturated Fat: 4g
- Cholesterol: 95mg
- Sodium: 280mg
- Total Carbohydrates: 7g
- Dietary Fiber: 1g
- Sugars: 2g
- Protein: 9g

**Ingredients:**
- 6 large eggs
- 1/4 cup milk
- 2 cups fresh spinach, chopped
- 1/2 cup crumbled feta cheese
- 1/4 cup diced onion
- 1/4 cup diced red bell pepper
- Salt and pepper to taste

**Directions:**
1. Preheat your oven to 350°F (175°C) and grease a muffin tin with cooking spray or line it with muffin liners.
2. In a large mixing bowl, whisk together the eggs and milk until well combined.
3. Add the chopped spinach, crumbled feta cheese, diced onion, and diced red bell pepper to the egg mixture. Season with salt and pepper to taste.
4. Mix all the ingredients until evenly distributed.
5. Pour the mixture evenly into the prepared muffin tin, filling each cup about 2/3 full.
6. Bake in the preheated oven for 20-25 minutes, or until the muffins are set and slightly golden on top.
7. Remove from the oven and allow the muffins to cool in the tin for a few minutes before transferring them to a wire rack to cool completely.
8. Once cooled, serve the Spinach and Feta Breakfast Muffins warm or at room temperature.

# BREAKFAST BURRITO WITH CAULIFLOWER TORTILLA

**Serving Size**: 2 burritos

Prep Time: 15 minutes
Cooking Time: 20 minutes

**Nutrition Info (per burrito):**
- Calories: 320
- Total Fat: 22g
- Saturated Fat: 8g
- Cholesterol: 230mg
- Sodium: 670mg
- Total Carbohydrates: 9g
- Dietary Fiber: 5g
- Sugars: 3g
- Protein: 24g

**Ingredients:**
- 2 large cauliflower tortillas (store-bought or homemade)
- 4 large eggs
- 1/4 cup diced bell pepper (any color)
- 1/4 cup diced onion
- 2 slices cooked bacon, crumbled
- 1/4 cup shredded cheddar cheese
- Salt and pepper to taste
- Avocado slices, salsa, or hot sauce for serving (optional)

**Directions**:
1. If using store-bought cauliflower tortillas, warm them according to the package instructions. If making homemade cauliflower tortillas, prepare them in advance.
2. In a skillet over medium heat, cook the diced bell pepper and onion until softened, about 3-4 minutes.
3. Push the veggies to one side of the skillet and crack the eggs into the empty side. Scramble the eggs until

cooked through, then mix them with the cooked vegetables.

4. Season the egg mixture with salt and pepper to taste.

5. Place half of the egg mixture in the center of each cauliflower tortilla.

6. Sprinkle half of the crumbled bacon and shredded cheddar cheese over each portion of the egg mixture.

7. Carefully fold the sides of the tortilla over the filling, then roll it up tightly to form a burrito.

8. Optional: If desired, lightly grill the assembled burritos in a skillet or grill pan for a few minutes on each side to crisp up the tortilla and melt the cheese further.

9. Serve the Keto Breakfast Burritos with avocado slices, salsa, or hot sauce on the side for extra flavor, if desired.

# SMOKED SALMON AND CREAM CHEESE ROLL-UPS

**Serving Size**: 4 roll-ups
Prep Time: 10 minutes
Cooking Time: 0 minutes (no cooking required)

**Nutrition Info (per roll-up):**
- Calories: 100
- Total Fat: 7g
- Saturated Fat: 3g
- Cholesterol: 15mg
- Sodium: 300mg
- Total Carbohydrates: 1g
- Dietary Fiber: 0g
- Sugars: 0g
- Protein: 8g

**Ingredients:**
- 4 slices smoked salmon
- 4 tablespoons cream cheese
- 1 tablespoon chopped fresh dill (optional)
- 1 teaspoon capers (optional)
- Fresh lemon wedges, for serving (optional)

**Directions**:
1. Lay out the smoked salmon slices on a clean work surface.
2. Spread 1 tablespoon of cream cheese evenly over each slice of smoked salmon.
3. If desired, sprinkle chopped fresh dill and capers evenly over the cream cheese.
4. Starting from one end, roll up each slice of smoked salmon tightly to form a roll-up.
5. Repeat with the remaining ingredients until all the roll-ups are assembled.
6. Optional: Slice each roll-up into bite-sized pieces for easy serving.
7. Serve the Smoked Salmon and Cream Cheese Roll-Ups with fresh lemon wedges on the side for squeezing over the roll-ups, if desired.

# CHAPTER 2
## SATISFYING STARTERS

## AVOCADO BACON BITES

**Serving Size**: 12 bites
Prep Time: 15 minutes
Cooking Time: 15 minutes

**Nutrition Info (per bite):**
- Calories: 80
- Total Fat: 6g
- Saturated Fat: 1.5g
- Cholesterol: 5mg
- Sodium: 100mg
- Total Carbohydrates: 3g
- Dietary Fiber: 2g
- Sugars: 0g
- Protein: 3g

**Ingredients:**
- 2 ripe avocados
- 6 slices bacon, cooked until crispy
- 1 tablespoon lemon juice
- 1/4 teaspoon garlic powder
- Salt and pepper to taste
- Toothpicks, for serving

**Directions:**
1. Cut the avocados in half and remove the pits. Scoop out the flesh into a bowl and mash it with a fork until smooth.
2. Crumble the cooked bacon slices and add them to the mashed avocado.
3. Add lemon juice, garlic powder, salt, and pepper to the avocado-bacon mixture. Mix well to combine all the ingredients.
4. Take small portions of the avocado mixture and roll them into bite-sized balls.
5. Place a toothpick in each avocado bacon bite for easy serving.
6. Optional: If desired, you can sprinkle additional lemon juice over the avocado bacon bites to prevent them from browning.
7. Serve the Avocado Bacon Bites as a delicious appetizer or snack option at your next gathering or enjoy them as a tasty treat any time of day!

# CAPRESE SALAD SKEWERS

**Serving Size**: 12 skewers
Prep Time: 15 minutes
Cooking Time: 0 minutes (no cooking required)

**Nutrition Info (per skewer):**
- Calories: 50
- Total Fat: 3.5g
- Saturated Fat: 1.5g
- Cholesterol: 5mg
- Sodium: 60mg
- Total Carbohydrates: 2g

- Dietary Fiber: 0g
- Sugars: 1g
- Protein: 3g

**Ingredients:**
- 12 cherry tomatoes
- 12 fresh mozzarella balls (bocconcini)
- 12 fresh basil leaves
- Balsamic glaze, for drizzling (optional)
- Salt and pepper to taste
- 12 small skewers or toothpicks

**Directions**:
1. Rinse the cherry tomatoes and pat them dry with paper towels.
2. Drain the mozzarella balls if they are stored in liquid, then pat them dry with paper towels.
3. To assemble each skewer, thread one cherry tomato, one mozzarella ball, and one basil leaf onto a skewer or toothpick. Repeat until all the skewers are assembled.
4. Arrange the Caprese Salad Skewers on a serving platter.
5. Optional: Just before serving, drizzle balsamic glaze over the skewers for an extra burst of flavor.
6. Season the skewers with salt and pepper to taste, if desired.
7. Serve the Caprese Salad Skewers as a delightful appetizer or light snack at your next gathering or enjoy them as a refreshing treat any time of day!

# GARLIC PARMESAN BAKED WINGS

**Serving Size**: 4 servings
Prep Time: 10 minutes
Cooking Time: 40 minutes

**Nutrition Info (per serving):**
- Calories: 320
- Total Fat: 20g
- Saturated Fat: 7g
- Cholesterol: 90mg
- Sodium: 780mg
- Total Carbohydrates: 6g
- Dietary Fiber: 0g
- Sugars: 0g
- Protein: 28g

**Ingredients:**
- 2 lbs chicken wings
- 2 tbsp olive oil
- 1 tsp salt
- 1 tsp black pepper
- 1 tsp garlic powder
- 1/2 cup grated Parmesan cheese
- 2 tbsp chopped fresh parsley
- 4 cloves garlic, minced
- 2 tbsp unsalted butter, melted

**Directions:**
1. Preheat your oven to 400°F (200°C) and line a baking sheet with parchment paper or aluminum foil.

2. In a large bowl, toss the chicken wings with olive oil, salt, pepper, and garlic powder until evenly coated.

3. Arrange the wings in a single layer on the prepared baking sheet and bake for 30-35 minutes, or until they are crispy and golden brown, flipping halfway through.

4. While the wings are baking, mix together the grated Parmesan cheese, chopped parsley, minced garlic, and melted butter in a small bowl.

5. Once the wings are cooked, remove them from the oven and immediately toss them in the garlic Parmesan mixture until evenly coated.

6. Serve the wings hot, garnished with extra Parmesan cheese and parsley if desired.

# ZUCCHINI FRITTERS WITH SOUR CREAM DIP

**Serving Size:** 4 servings
Prep Time: 15 minutes
Cooking Time: 15 minutes

**Nutrition Info (per serving):**
- Calories: 190
- Total Fat: 11g
- Saturated Fat: 4g
- Cholesterol: 55mg
- Sodium: 380mg
- Total Carbohydrates: 18g
- Dietary Fiber: 2g
- Sugars: 3g
- Protein: 6g

**Ingredients:**
For Zucchini Fritters:
- 2 medium zucchinis, grated
- 1/2 teaspoon salt
- 1/4 cup all-purpose flour
- 1/4 cup grated Parmesan cheese
- 1/4 cup chopped fresh parsley
- 1/4 cup chopped green onions
- 1 large egg, beaten
- 2 cloves garlic, minced
- 2 tablespoons olive oil

**For Sour Cream Dip:**
- 1/2 cup sour cream
- 1 tablespoon lemon juice
- 1/2 teaspoon garlic powder
- Salt and pepper to taste

**Directions:**
1. Start by preparing the zucchini. Place the grated zucchini in a colander, sprinkle with salt, and let it sit for about 10 minutes to allow excess moisture to drain. Afterward, squeeze out any remaining liquid using a clean kitchen towel.
2. In a large mixing bowl, combine the grated zucchini, flour, Parmesan cheese, parsley, green onions, beaten egg, and minced garlic. Mix well until all ingredients are evenly incorporated.
3. Heat olive oil in a skillet over medium heat. Once the oil is hot, spoon about 2 tablespoons of the zucchini mixture into the skillet, flattening slightly to form fritters. Cook for 3-4 minutes on each side, or until golden brown and crispy. Repeat this process with the remaining zucchini mixture, adding more oil to the skillet as needed.
4. While the fritters are cooking, prepare the sour cream dip. In a small bowl, mix together sour cream, lemon juice,

garlic powder, salt, and pepper until well combined. Adjust seasoning to taste.

5. Once the zucchini fritters are cooked, transfer them to a plate lined with paper towels to drain any excess oil.

6. Serve the warm zucchini fritters with the tangy sour cream dip on the side. Enjoy these crispy

# KETO STUFFED MUSHROOMS

**Serving Size**: 4 servings
Prep Time: 15 minutes
Cooking Time: 20 minutes

**Nutrition Info (per serving):**
- Calories: 150
- Total Fat: 12g
- Saturated Fat: 5g
- Cholesterol: 25mg
- Sodium: 280mg
- Total Carbohydrates: 4g
- Dietary Fiber: 1g
- Sugars: 2g
- Protein: 7g

**Ingredients:**
- 12 large mushrooms, stems removed and reserved
- 1 tablespoon olive oil
- 2 cloves garlic, minced
- 4 ounces cream cheese, softened
- 1/4 cup grated Parmesan cheese
- 2 tablespoons chopped fresh parsley
- Salt and pepper to taste
- 1/4 cup shredded mozzarella cheese

**Directions**:
1. Preheat your oven to 375°F (190°C) and line a baking sheet with parchment paper.
2. Clean the mushrooms and remove the stems. Finely chop the reserved mushroom stems.
3. Heat olive oil in a skillet over medium heat. Add minced garlic and chopped mushroom stems, and sauté until softened, about 3-4 minutes. Remove from heat and let it cool slightly.
4. In a mixing bowl, combine the softened cream cheese, grated Parmesan cheese, chopped parsley, salt, pepper, and the sautéed garlic and mushroom mixture. Mix until well combined.
5. Stuff each mushroom cap generously with the cream cheese mixture, mounding it slightly.
6. Place the stuffed mushrooms on the prepared baking sheet. Sprinkle shredded mozzarella cheese on top of each stuffed mushroom.
7. Bake in the preheated oven for 15-20 minutes, or until the mushrooms are tender and the cheese is melted and bubbly.
8. Remove from the oven and let the stuffed mushrooms cool for a few minutes before serving.
9. Enjoy these keto stuffed mushrooms as a delicious appetizer or side dish! They are packed with flavor and perfect for anyone following a low-carb or keto diet.

# CUCUMBER AND CREAM CHEESE ROLL-UPS

**Serving Size**: 4 servings
Prep Time: 10 minutes
Cooking Time: 0 minutes

**Nutrition Info (per serving):**
- Calories: 70
- Total Fat: 6g
- Saturated Fat: 3.5g
- Cholesterol: 20mg
- Sodium: 110mg
- Total Carbohydrates: 2g
- Dietary Fiber: 0g
- Sugars: 1g
- Protein: 2g

**Ingredients**:
- 1 large cucumber
- 4 ounces cream cheese, softened
- 2 tablespoons finely chopped fresh dill (optional)
- Salt and pepper to taste

**Directions**:
1. Start by preparing the cucumber. Wash it thoroughly and pat it dry with a paper towel. Using a vegetable peeler, peel thin strips lengthwise along the cucumber to create long, thin slices.
2. In a small bowl, mix the softened cream cheese with chopped fresh dill, if using. Season with salt and pepper to taste.
3. Lay out the cucumber slices on a clean work surface. Spread a thin layer of the cream cheese mixture onto each cucumber slice, covering it evenly.
4. Carefully roll up each cucumber slice with the cream cheese filling inside, starting from one end and rolling tightly to the other end.
5. Secure the roll-ups with toothpicks if necessary to keep them from unraveling.

6. Repeat the process until all cucumber slices are rolled up with the cream cheese filling.

7. Arrange the cucumber and cream cheese roll-ups on a serving platter and serve immediately, or refrigerate until ready to serve.

8. Enjoy these refreshing and low-carb cucumber and cream cheese roll-ups as a healthy snack or appetizer! They're perfect for a light and satisfying bite any time of day.

# CHAPTER 3
## SCRUMPTIOUS SALADS

## COBB SALAD WITH RANCH DRESSING

**Serving Size**: 4 servings
Prep Time: 20 minutes
Cooking Time: 10 minutes

**Nutrition Info (per serving):**
- Calories: 380
- Total Fat: 28g
- Saturated Fat: 8g
- Cholesterol: 180mg
- Sodium: 760mg
- Total Carbohydrates: 9g
- Dietary Fiber: 3g
- Sugars: 4g
- Protein: 23g

**Ingredients:**
For Cobb Salad:
- 4 cups chopped romaine lettuce
- 2 cups chopped cooked chicken breast
- 4 slices cooked bacon, crumbled
- 2 hard-boiled eggs, chopped
- 1 avocado, diced
- 1 cup cherry tomatoes, halved

- 1/2 cup crumbled blue cheese
- Salt and pepper to taste
For Ranch Dressing:
- 1/2 cup mayonnaise
- 1/4 cup sour cream
- 2 tablespoons chopped fresh chives
- 1 tablespoon chopped fresh parsley
- 1 clove garlic, minced
- 1 teaspoon Dijon mustard
- 1 teaspoon lemon juice
- Salt and pepper to taste
- 2 tablespoons milk (optional, for thinning)

**Directions**:
1. Start by preparing the ingredients for the Cobb Salad. Wash and chop the romaine lettuce, cooked chicken breast, bacon slices, hard-boiled eggs, avocado, and cherry tomatoes. Crumble the blue cheese.
2. In a large salad bowl, layer the chopped romaine lettuce as the base.
3. Arrange the chopped cooked chicken breast, crumbled bacon, chopped hard-boiled eggs, diced avocado, halved cherry tomatoes, and crumbled blue cheese in rows on top of the romaine lettuce.
4. Season the Cobb Salad with salt and pepper to taste.
5. To make the Ranch Dressing, in a small bowl, whisk together mayonnaise, sour cream, chopped fresh chives, chopped fresh parsley, minced garlic, Dijon mustard, lemon juice, salt, and pepper until well combined. If desired, thin out the dressing with milk to achieve the desired consistency.
6. Drizzle the Ranch Dressing over the Cobb Salad just before serving, or serve it on the side.
7. Toss the salad gently to coat evenly with the dressing.

8. Serve the Cobb Salad with Ranch Dressing immediately as a delicious and satisfying meal or appetizer. Enjoy the combination of fresh ingredients and creamy dressing in this classic salad!

# GREEK SALAD WITH FETA AND OLIVES

**Serving Size**: 4 servings
Prep Time: 15 minutes
Cooking Time: 0 minutes

**Nutrition Info (per serving)**:
- Calories: 220
- Total Fat: 18g
- Saturated Fat: 6g
- Cholesterol: 25mg
- Sodium: 520mg
- Total Carbohydrates: 10g
- Dietary Fiber: 3g
- Sugars: 6g
- Protein: 6g

**Ingredients:**
- 4 cups chopped romaine lettuce
- 1 cucumber, diced
- 1 cup cherry tomatoes, halved
- 1/2 red onion, thinly sliced
- 1/2 cup Kalamata olives, pitted
- 1/2 cup crumbled feta cheese
- 2 tablespoons chopped fresh parsley
- Salt and pepper to taste
- 2 tablespoons extra virgin olive oil

- 1 tablespoon red wine vinegar
- 1 teaspoon dried oregano

**Directions**:
1. Start by preparing the ingredients for the Greek Salad. Wash and chop the romaine lettuce, cucumber, cherry tomatoes, and red onion. Pit the Kalamata olives if they aren't already pitted. Crumble the feta cheese.
2. In a large salad bowl, combine the chopped romaine lettuce, diced cucumber, halved cherry tomatoes, thinly sliced red onion, pitted Kalamata olives, crumbled feta cheese, and chopped fresh parsley.
3. Season the salad with salt and pepper to taste.
4. In a small bowl, whisk together the extra virgin olive oil, red wine vinegar, and dried oregano until well combined to make the dressing.
5. Drizzle the dressing over the Greek Salad ingredients in the salad bowl.
6. Gently toss the salad to coat evenly with the dressing.
7. Serve the Greek Salad with Feta and Olives immediately as a refreshing and flavorful side dish or light meal. Enjoy the vibrant flavors and textures of this classic Mediterranean salad!

# CAESAR SALAD WITH GRILLED CHICKEN

**Serving Size:** 4 servings
Prep Time: 15 minutes
Cooking Time: 15 minutes

**Nutrition Info (per serving):**
- Calories: 320

- Total Fat: 18g
- Saturated Fat: 4g
- Cholesterol: 85mg
- Sodium: 780mg
- Total Carbohydrates: 10g
- Dietary Fiber: 3g
- Sugars: 2g
- Protein: 30g

**Ingredients:**
For Caesar Salad:
- 1 head romaine lettuce, chopped
- 1/2 cup grated Parmesan cheese
- 1 cup croutons
- Caesar dressing (store-bought or homemade)
- Salt and pepper to taste
For Grilled Chicken:
- 2 boneless, skinless chicken breasts
- 2 tablespoons olive oil
- 1 teaspoon garlic powder
- 1 teaspoon dried oregano
- Salt and pepper to taste

**Directions:**
1. Start by preparing the ingredients for the Caesar Salad. Wash and chop the romaine lettuce, grate the Parmesan cheese, and gather the croutons.
2. Season the chicken breasts with olive oil, garlic powder, dried oregano, salt, and pepper. Make sure the chicken is evenly coated with the seasonings.
3. Preheat your grill or grill pan over medium-high heat. Grill the seasoned chicken breasts for 6-8 minutes per side, or until they are cooked through and have nice grill marks. Remove from the grill and let them rest for a few minutes before slicing.

4. While the chicken is grilling, assemble the Caesar Salad. In a large salad bowl, combine the chopped romaine lettuce, grated Parmesan cheese, and croutons.
5. Once the chicken has rested, slice it into thin strips.
6. Add the sliced grilled chicken to the salad bowl.
7. Drizzle the Caesar dressing over the salad ingredients, starting with a small amount and adding more as needed to coat the salad evenly. Toss the salad gently to combine all the ingredients.
8. Season the Caesar Salad with salt and pepper to taste.
9. Serve the Caesar Salad with Grilled Chicken immediately as a satisfying and flavorful meal.

# SHRIMP AVOCADO SALAD WITH LEMON VINAIGRETTE

**Serving Size**
- Serves: 4
Prep Time
- 15 minutes
Cooking Time
- 5 minutes
Total Time
- 20 minutes

**Nutrition Information (per serving)**
- Calories: 250
- Protein: 18g
- Carbohydrates: 12g
- Fat: 15g
- Fiber: 6g
- Sodium: 450mg

## Ingredients
- 1 lb large shrimp, peeled and deveined
- 2 ripe avocados, diced
- 1 cup cherry tomatoes, halved
- 1 small red onion, thinly sliced
- 1 cucumber, diced
- 1 cup mixed greens or arugula
- 2 tbsp olive oil
- 1 lemon, juiced
- 1 tsp Dijon mustard
- 1 tsp honey
- Salt and pepper to taste
- Fresh cilantro or parsley, chopped (optional, for garnish)

## Directions
1. Cook the Shrimp:
- Heat a large skillet over medium-high heat. Add 1 tablespoon of olive oil.
- Season the shrimp with salt and pepper.
- Cook the shrimp for about 2-3 minutes on each side until they turn pink and opaque.
Remove from the heat and let cool slightly.
2. Prepare the Lemon Vinaigrette:
- In a small bowl, whisk together the lemon juice, remaining olive oil, Dijon mustard, honey, salt, and pepper until well combined.
3. Assemble the Salad:
- In a large salad bowl, combine the diced avocados, cherry tomatoes, red onion, cucumber, and mixed greens.
- Add the cooked shrimp to the salad.
4. Dress the Salad:
- Drizzle the lemon vinaigrette over the salad.

- Toss gently to combine, making sure all ingredients are coated with the dressing.
5. Garnish and Serve:
- Garnish with fresh cilantro or parsley if desired.
- Serve immediately and enjoy your refreshing Shrimp **Avocado Salad with Lemon Vinaigrette!**
This light and nutritious salad is perfect for a quick lunch or a healthy dinner, bursting with fresh flavors and ready in just 20 minutes.

# BROCCOLI SALAD WITH BACON AND CHEDDAR

**Ingredients**:
- 4 cups fresh broccoli florets
- 6 slices bacon, cooked and crumbled
- 1 cup shredded cheddar cheese
- 1/2 cup red onion, finely chopped
- 1/2 cup sunflower seeds
- 1/2 cup dried cranberries
For the Dressing:
- 1 cup mayonnaise
- 2 tablespoons apple cider vinegar
- 2 tablespoons sugar
- Salt and pepper to taste

**Directions**:
1. Prep the Ingredients: Wash and chop the broccoli into bite-sized florets. Cook the bacon until crispy, then crumble it into small pieces. Shred the cheddar cheese and finely chop the red onion.

2. Make the Dressing: In a small bowl, whisk together the mayonnaise, apple cider vinegar, sugar, salt, and pepper until smooth and well combined.
3. Assemble the Salad: In a large bowl, combine the broccoli, crumbled bacon, shredded cheddar cheese, chopped red onion, sunflower seeds, and dried cranberries.
4. Add the Dressing: Pour the dressing over the salad and toss until all the ingredients are evenly coated.
5. Chill and Serve: Cover the salad and refrigerate for at least 1 hour before serving to allow the flavors to meld together. Serve chilled.

## Serving Size:
This recipe serves approximately 6-8 people as a side dish.
Prep Time:
15 minutes
Cooking Time:
15 minutes (for cooking the bacon)
Total Time:
30 minutes

## Nutrition Information (per serving):
- Calories: 320
- Protein: 8g
- Carbohydrates: 12g
- Dietary Fiber: 3g
- Sugars: 8g
- Fat: 28g
- Saturated Fat: 7g
- Cholesterol: 30mg
- Sodium: 450mg

**Tips**:
- For a lighter version, you can substitute the mayonnaise with Greek yogurt.
- Feel free to add other ingredients like cherry tomatoes, shredded carrots, or even some
chopped nuts for extra crunch.
- If you prefer, you can use turkey bacon or vegetarian bacon alternatives.

# SPINACH SALAD WITH STRAWBERRIES AND BALSAMIC DRESSING

### Serving Size
This recipe serves 4.
Cooking and Prep Time
- Prep Time: 15 minutes
- Cook Time: None
- Total Time: 15 minutes

### Nutrition Information (per serving)
- Calories: 150
- Protein: 3g
- Carbohydrates: 15g
- Fat: 9g
- Fiber: 3g
- Sugar: 10g

### Ingredients
- 6 cups fresh spinach leaves, washed and dried
- 1 pint strawberries, hulled and sliced
- 1/4 cup sliced almonds, toasted

- 1/4 cup crumbled feta cheese (optional)
- 1/4 red onion, thinly sliced (optional)
For the Balsamic Dressing:
- 1/4 cup balsamic vinegar
- 2 tablespoons honey or maple syrup
- 1/2 teaspoon Dijon mustard
- 1/2 cup extra-virgin olive oil
- Salt and freshly ground black pepper, to taste

**Directions**
1. Prepare the Dressing:
- In a small bowl or a jar with a tight-fitting lid, combine the balsamic vinegar, honey (or maple syrup), and Dijon mustard.
- Gradually whisk in the olive oil until the dressing is well blended and emulsified.
- Season with salt and freshly ground black pepper to taste. Set aside.
2. Assemble the Salad:
- In a large salad bowl, combine the spinach leaves and sliced strawberries.
- Add the sliced almonds, and if using, sprinkle the feta cheese and red onion on top.
3. Dress the Salad:
- Drizzle the prepared balsamic dressing over the salad just before serving.
- Gently toss the salad to ensure all ingredients are evenly coated with the dressing.
4. Serve:
- Divide the salad among four plates.
- Serve immediately and enjoy the refreshing blend of flavors.

**Tips**
- Variations: Feel free to add other ingredients like sliced avocado, grilled chicken, or quinoa for added texture and protein.
- Storage: Store any leftover dressing in the refrigerator for up to a week. The salad is best enjoyed fresh but can be stored without dressing in an airtight container for up to two days.

# CHAPTER 4

## FLAVORFUL MAIN COURSES

## GARLIC BUTTER SHRIMP WITH ZUCCHINI NOODLES

**Serving Size**
This recipe serves 4.
Prep Time
15 minutes
Cooking Time
10 minutes

**Nutrition Information (per serving)**
- Calories: 250
- Protein: 25g
- Fat: 15g
- Carbohydrates: 6g
- Fiber: 2g

**Ingredients**
- 1 lb (450g) large shrimp, peeled and deveined
- 4 medium zucchini, spiralized into noodles
- 3 tablespoons butter
- 4 cloves garlic, minced
- 1/4 teaspoon red pepper flakes (optional)
- Salt and black pepper, to taste
- 1 tablespoon lemon juice
- 2 tablespoons fresh parsley, chopped

- 1/4 cup grated Parmesan cheese (optional)

**Directions**
1. Prepare the Zucchini Noodles: Use a spiralizer to turn the zucchini into noodles. Set aside.
2. Cook the Shrimp: In a large skillet, melt 2 tablespoons of butter over medium-high heat. Add the shrimp, garlic, and red pepper flakes. Season with salt and black pepper. Cook for about 2-3
minutes on each side until the shrimp is pink and opaque. Remove the shrimp from the skillet and set aside.
3. Cook the Zucchini Noodles: In the same skillet, add the remaining tablespoon of butter. Add the zucchini noodles and sauté for 2-3 minutes until just tender but still crisp.
4. Combine and Finish: Return the shrimp to the skillet with the zucchini noodles. Add the lemon juice and parsley. Toss everything together and cook for another minute until heated through.
5. Serve: Transfer to plates and, if desired, sprinkle with grated Parmesan cheese before serving.

# CREAMY TUSCAN CHICKEN

**Serving Size:**
4 servings
Prep Time:
10 minutes
Cooking Time:
25 minutes
Total Time:
35 minutes

**Nutrition Information (per serving):**
- Calories: 450

- Protein: 34g
- Carbohydrates: 6g
- Fat: 31g
- Fiber: 1g

## Ingredients:
- 4 boneless, skinless chicken breasts
- Salt and pepper, to taste
- 1 tablespoon olive oil
- 1 tablespoon butter
- 3 cloves garlic, minced
- 1 cup heavy cream
- 1/2 cup chicken broth
- 1/2 cup grated Parmesan cheese
- 1 teaspoon Italian seasoning
- 1 cup sun-dried tomatoes (in oil), drained and chopped
- 2 cups fresh spinach

## Directions:
1. Prepare the Chicken:
- Season the chicken breasts with salt and pepper on both sides.
2. Cook the Chicken:
- Heat olive oil in a large skillet over medium-high heat.
- Add the chicken breasts and cook for about 5-7 minutes on each side, until golden brown and cooked through.
- Remove the chicken from the skillet and set aside.
3. Make the Sauce:
- In the same skillet, add the butter and let it melt.
- Add the minced garlic and sauté for about 1 minute until fragrant.
- Pour in the heavy cream and chicken broth, stirring to combine.
- Bring the mixture to a gentle simmer.
4. Add Cheese and Seasoning:

- Stir in the grated Parmesan cheese and Italian seasoning until the cheese is melted and the sauce is smooth.
5. Incorporate Vegetables:
- Add the sun-dried tomatoes and fresh spinach to the skillet.
- Cook, stirring occasionally, until the spinach is wilted, about 2-3 minutes.
6. Combine Chicken and Sauce:
- Return the cooked chicken breasts to the skillet, spooning the creamy sauce over them.
- Let everything simmer together for an additional 5 minutes to allow the flavors to meld.
7. Serve:
- Serve the Creamy Tuscan Chicken hot, with the sauce generously ladled over the chicken.
- It pairs well with pasta, rice, or a side of steamed vegetables.

# BEEF AND BROCCOLI STIR-FRY

**Serving Size**: 4 servings
Prep Time: 15 minutes
Cooking Time: 15 minutes

**Nutrition Info (per serving):**
- Calories: 320
- Total Fat: 15g
- Cholesterol: 55mg
- Sodium: 780mg
- Total Carbohydrates: 18g
- Dietary Fiber: 4g
- Sugars: 7g
- Protein: 29g

## Ingredients:
- 1 lb flank steak, thinly sliced
- 1 head broccoli, cut into florets
- 1/4 cup soy sauce
- 2 tablespoons oyster sauce
- 2 tablespoons hoisin sauce
- 1 tablespoon cornstarch
- 1 tablespoon vegetable oil
- 3 cloves garlic, minced
- 1 teaspoon ginger, minced
- 1/2 teaspoon red pepper flakes (optional)
- Cooked rice, for serving

## Directions:
1. In a bowl, combine soy sauce, oyster sauce, hoisin sauce, and cornstarch. Add sliced flank steak and marinate for 10 minutes.
2. Heat vegetable oil in a large skillet or wok over medium-high heat. Add minced garlic, ginger,and red pepper flakes. Stir-fry for 30 seconds.
3. Add the marinated beef to the skillet. Stir-fry until browned and cooked through, about 3-4 minutes.
4. Add broccoli florets to the skillet. Stir-fry for an additional 2-3 minutes or until broccoli is tender-crisp.
5. Serve the beef and broccoli stir-fry over cooked rice. Enjoy your flavorful and nutritious meal!

# BAKED LEMON HERB SALMON

**Serving Size**: 4 servings
Cooking Time: 20-25 minutes
Prep Time: 10 minutes

**Nutrition Info (per serving):**
Calories: 280
Protein: 29g
Carbohydrates: 3g
Fat: 16g
Saturated Fat: 3g
Cholesterol: 80mg
Sodium: 450mg
Potassium: 670mg
Fiber: 1g
Sugar: 1g
Vitamin A: 10%
Vitamin C: 15%
Calcium: 4%
Iron: 8%

**Ingredients**:
- 4 salmon fillets (about 6 ounces each)
- Salt and pepper to taste
- 2 tablespoons olive oil
- 2 tablespoons fresh lemon juice
- 2 cloves garlic, minced
- 1 teaspoon dried thyme
- 1 teaspoon dried rosemary
- 1 teaspoon dried oregano
- 1 teaspoon paprika
- Fresh parsley, chopped (for garnish)
- Lemon slices (for garnish)

**Directions:**
1. Preheat your oven to 400°F (200°C) and line a baking sheet with parchment paper.
2. Place the salmon fillets on the prepared baking sheet. Season both sides with salt and pepper.

3. In a small bowl, mix together the olive oil, lemon juice, minced garlic, dried thyme, dried
rosemary, dried oregano, and paprika.
4. Brush the herb mixture over the salmon fillets, covering them evenly.
5. Place a few lemon slices on top of each fillet for extra flavor.
6. Bake the salmon in the preheated oven for 20-25 minutes, or until the fish flakes easily with a fork.
7. Once done, remove the salmon from the oven and let it rest for a few minutes.
8. Garnish with fresh chopped parsley before serving.
9. Enjoy your delicious and healthy Baked Lemon Herb Salmon

# STUFFED BELL PEPPERS

**Serving Size**: 4
Prep Time: 20 minutes
Cooking Time: 40 minutes

**Nutrition Info: (Per serving)**
- Calories: 320
- Total Fat: 14g
- Cholesterol: 45mg
- Sodium: 680mg
- Total Carbohydrates: 32g
- Dietary Fiber: 6g
- Sugars: 10g
- Protein: 18g

**Ingredients**:
- 4 large bell peppers (any color)

- 1 pound ground beef
- 1 cup cooked rice
- 1 can (14 ounces) diced tomatoes, drained
- 1 cup shredded cheddar cheese
- 1 small onion, finely chopped
- 2 cloves garlic, minced
- 1 teaspoon dried oregano
- 1 teaspoon dried basil
- Salt and pepper to taste
- Olive oil

**Directions**:
1. Preheat Oven: Preheat your oven to 375°F (190°C).
2. Prepare Peppers: Cut the tops off the bell peppers and remove the seeds and membranes.
Rinse the peppers under cold water and set them aside.
3. Cook Beef Mixture: In a large skillet, heat a drizzle of olive oil over medium heat. Add the chopped onion and garlic, and cook until softened and fragrant, about 3-4 minutes. Add the ground beef and cook until browned, breaking it apart with a spoon as it cooks. Drain excess fat if needed.
4. Mix Ingredients: In a large mixing bowl, combine the cooked ground beef mixture, cooked rice, diced tomatoes, shredded cheddar cheese, dried oregano, dried basil, salt, and pepper. Mix everything well.
5. Stuff Peppers: Place the bell peppers upright in a baking dish. Stuff each pepper with the beef and rice mixture, pressing it down gently to fill the peppers evenly.
6. Bake: Cover the baking dish with aluminum foil and bake in the preheated oven for about 30 minutes. Then remove the foil and bake for an additional 10 minutes, or until the peppers are tender and the filling is heated through.

7. Serve: Once done, remove the stuffed peppers from the oven and let them cool slightly before serving. Garnish with chopped fresh herbs like parsley or cilantro if desired.

# EGGPLANT LASAGNA

**Serving Size**: 6
Prep Time: 30 minutes
Cooking Time: 1 hour

**Nutrition Info: (Per serving)**
- Calories: 320
- Total Fat: 18g
- Cholesterol: 45mg
- Sodium: 680mg
- Total Carbohydrates: 25g
- Dietary Fiber: 6g
- Sugars: 10g
- Protein: 16g

**Ingredients:**
- 2 medium eggplants, sliced lengthwise into 1/4-inch thick slices
- 1 pound ground beef or turkey
- 1 onion, chopped
- 3 cloves garlic, minced
- 1 can (14 ounces) crushed tomatoes
- 1 can (6 ounces) tomato paste
- 1 teaspoon dried basil
- 1 teaspoon dried oregano
- Salt and pepper to taste
- 2 cups shredded mozzarella cheese
- 1 cup grated Parmesan cheese

- Olive oil
- Fresh basil or parsley for garnish (optional)

**Directions**:
1. Preheat Oven: Preheat your oven to 375°F (190°C).
2. Prepare Eggplant: Place the eggplant slices on a baking sheet lined with parchment paper. Drizzle olive oil over the slices and sprinkle with salt and pepper. Bake in the preheated oven for
about 15-20 minutes, or until the eggplant slices are tender. Remove from the oven and set aside.
3. Cook Meat Sauce: In a large skillet, heat a drizzle of olive oil over medium heat. Add the
chopped onion and garlic, and cook until softened and fragrant, about 3-4 minutes. Add the ground beef or turkey and cook until browned, breaking it apart with a spoon as it cooks. Drain excess fat if needed. Stir in the crushed tomatoes, tomato paste, dried basil, dried oregano, salt, and pepper. Simmer for 10-15 minutes, allowing the flavors to meld.
4. Assemble Lasagna: In a greased 9x13-inch baking dish, spread a thin layer of the meat sauce on the bottom. Arrange a layer of baked eggplant slices on top of the sauce. Sprinkle some shredded mozzarella and grated Parmesan cheese over the eggplant. Repeat the layers until all ingredients are used, ending with a layer of cheese on top.
5. Bake: Cover the baking dish with aluminum foil and bake in the preheated oven for about 30 minutes. Then remove the foil and bake for an additional 15 minutes, or until the cheese is bubbly and golden.
6. Serve: Once done, remove the eggplant lasagna from the oven and let it cool slightly before
slicing. Garnish with fresh basil or parsley if desired.

# CHAPTER 5

## DELECTABLE SIDE DISHES:

## GARLIC PARMESAN ROASTED BRUSSELS SPROUTS

**Serving Size: 4**
Prep Time: 10 minutes
Cooking Time: 20 minutes

**Nutrition Info: (Per serving)**
- Calories: 150
- Total Fat: 9g
- Cholesterol: 5mg
- Sodium: 250mg
- Total Carbohydrates: 14g
- Dietary Fiber: 5g
- Sugars: 3g
- Protein: 7g

**Ingredients:**
- 1 pound Brussels sprouts, trimmed and halved
- 2 tablespoons olive oil
- 2 cloves garlic, minced
- 1/4 cup grated Parmesan cheese
- Salt and pepper to taste
- Optional: red pepper flakes for a spicy kick

**Directions**:
1. Preheat Oven: Preheat your oven to 400°F (200°C).
2. Prepare Brussels Sprouts: Trim the ends off the Brussels sprouts and cut them in half. Place them in a large mixing bowl.
3. Seasoning Mixture: In a small bowl, combine the olive oil, minced garlic, grated Parmesan cheese, salt, pepper, and optional red pepper flakes. Mix well to form a seasoning mixture.
4. Coat Brussels Sprouts: Pour the seasoning mixture over the Brussels sprouts in the mixing bowl. Toss well to ensure that all the sprouts are evenly coated with the mixture.
5. Roast: Spread the Brussels sprouts in a single layer on a baking sheet lined with parchment paper or aluminum foil. Roast in the preheated oven for about 20 minutes or until the sprouts are tender and lightly browned, stirring halfway through cooking.
6. Serve: Once roasted to perfection, remove the Brussels sprouts from the oven and transfer them to a serving dish. Garnish with additional grated Parmesan cheese if desired.

# CHEESY CAULIFLOWER RICE

**Serving Size**: 4
Prep Time: 10 minutes
Cooking Time: 15 minutes

**Nutrition Info: (Per serving)**
- Calories: 180
- Total Fat: 12g
- Cholesterol: 25mg
- Sodium: 380mg

- Total Carbohydrates: 10g
- Dietary Fiber: 3g
- Sugars: 4g
- Protein: 9g

**Ingredients**:
- 1 medium head of cauliflower, grated (about 4 cups)
- 1 tablespoon olive oil
- 2 cloves garlic, minced
- 1/2 cup shredded cheddar cheese
- 1/4 cup grated Parmesan cheese
- Salt and pepper to taste
- Chopped fresh parsley for garnish (optional)

**Directions**:
1. Prepare Cauliflower: Wash the cauliflower head thoroughly and remove the leaves and stem. Cut it into florets, and then grate the florets using a box grater or a food processor until you have about 4 cups of cauliflower rice.
2. Cook Cauliflower Rice: In a large skillet, heat the olive oil over medium heat. Add the minced garlic and sauté for about 1 minute until fragrant. Add the grated cauliflower to the skillet and cook, stirring frequently, for about 5-7 minutes until the cauliflower is tender but still slightly crisp.
3. Add Cheese: Reduce the heat to low. Add the shredded cheddar cheese and grated Parmesan cheese to the cauliflower rice. Stir well until the cheese melts and coats the cauliflower evenly. Season with salt and pepper to taste.
4. Serve: Remove the skillet from heat. Transfer the cheesy cauliflower rice to a serving dish. Garnish with chopped fresh parsley if desired.

# ZUCCHINI NOODLES WITH PESTO

**Serving Size**: 2
Prep Time: 15 minutes
Cooking Time: 10 minutes

**Nutrition Info: (Per serving)**
- Calories: 250
- Total Fat: 20g
- Cholesterol: 5mg
- Sodium: 280mg
- Total Carbohydrates: 15g
- Dietary Fiber: 5g
- Sugars: 5g
- Protein: 5g

**Ingredients**:
- 2 medium-sized zucchinis
- 1/2 cup basil leaves
- 1/4 cup grated Parmesan cheese
- 1/4 cup pine nuts
- 2 cloves garlic, minced
- 1/4 cup extra virgin olive oil
- Salt and pepper to taste
- Cherry tomatoes (optional, for garnish)

**Directions**:
1. Prepare Zucchini Noodles: Use a spiralizer or a vegetable peeler to create zucchini noodles (also known as zoodles) from the zucchinis. Set the zoodles aside on a paper towel to absorb excess moisture.
2. Make Pesto: In a food processor, combine the basil leaves, grated Parmesan cheese, pine nuts, minced garlic, salt, and pepper. Pulse until the ingredients are

finely chopped. While the processor is running, drizzle in the olive oil slowly until the pesto reaches a smooth consistency. Adjust seasoning as needed.

3. Cook Zoodles: Heat a tablespoon of olive oil in a large skillet over medium heat. Add the zucchini noodles and sauté for about 3-4 minutes until they are just tender but still have a slight crunch.

4. Combine Zoodles and Pesto: Once the zoodles are cooked, add the pesto sauce to the skillet. Toss the zucchini noodles gently to coat them evenly with the pesto sauce. Cook for another 1-2 minutes until heated through.

5. Serve: Divide the zucchini noodles with pesto between two serving plates. Garnish with halved cherry tomatoes if desired. Serve immediately and enjoy your healthy and flavorful zucchini noodle dish!

# CREAMED SPINACH

**Serving Size**: 4
Prep Time: 10 minutes
Cooking Time: 15 minutes

**Nutrition Info: (Per serving)**
- Calories: 180
- Total Fat: 13g
- Cholesterol: 30mg
- Sodium: 380mg
- Total Carbohydrates: 10g
- Dietary Fiber: 3g
- Sugars: 3g
- Protein: 7g

**Ingredients**:

- 1 pound fresh spinach, washed and stems removed
- 2 tablespoons butter
- 2 tablespoons all-purpose flour
- 1 cup milk (you can use whole milk or a milk alternative like almond milk)
- 1/2 cup heavy cream
- 1/4 cup grated Parmesan cheese
- 2 cloves garlic, minced
- Salt and pepper to taste
- A pinch of nutmeg (optional)

**Directions**:
1. Prepare Spinach: Start by washing the spinach thoroughly and removing any tough stems. You can leave the tender stems on.
2. Cook Spinach: In a large pot, bring some water to a boil. Add the spinach and blanch for about 1-2 minutes until wilted. Drain the spinach and rinse it under cold water to stop the cooking process. Squeeze out excess water from the spinach and chop it coarsely.
3. Make Cream Sauce: In a saucepan, melt the butter over medium heat. Add the minced garlic and sauté until fragrant, about 1 minute. Sprinkle the flour over the butter and garlic mixture, stirring constantly to create a roux. Cook the roux for about 2 minutes until it turns golden brown.
4. Add Liquid Ingredients: Slowly pour in the milk and heavy cream, whisking continuously to prevent lumps from forming. Bring the mixture to a simmer and let it cook until it thickens, about 3-4 minutes.
5. Combine Ingredients: Stir in the grated Parmesan cheese until melted and incorporated into the sauce. Season with salt, pepper, and a pinch of nutmeg if using.
6. Add Spinach: Add the chopped spinach to the cream sauce, stirring well to coat the spinach evenly with the

sauce. Let it cook for another 2-3 minutes until the spinach is heated through.

7. Serve: Remove the creamed spinach from heat and transfer it to a serving dish. Garnish with a sprinkle of additional Parmesan cheese if desired.

# BACON-WRAPPED ASPARAGUS

**Serving Size:** 4
Prep Time: 10 minutes
Cooking Time: 15 minutes

**Nutrition Info: (Per serving)**
- Calories: 180
- Total Fat: 12g
- Cholesterol: 25mg
- Sodium: 400mg
- Total Carbohydrates: 4g
- Dietary Fiber: 2g
- Sugars: 2g
- Protein: 13g

**Ingredients:**
- 1 bunch fresh asparagus spears
- 8 slices of bacon
- Olive oil
- Salt and pepper to taste
- Optional: grated Parmesan cheese

**Directions**:
1. Preheat Oven: Preheat your oven to 400°F (200°C).
2. Prepare Asparagus: Wash the asparagus spears and trim off the tough ends.

3. Wrap Asparagus: Take 4 asparagus spears and bundle them together. Wrap 2 slices of bacon around each bundle, securing the ends with toothpicks if needed. Repeat for the remaining asparagus spears.

4. Season: Place the bacon-wrapped asparagus bundles on a baking sheet. Drizzle with a little olive oil and season with salt and pepper to taste. For extra flavor, you can sprinkle grated Parmesan cheese over the bundles.

5. Bake: Bake in the preheated oven for about 15 minutes or until the bacon is crispy and the asparagus is tender.

6. Serve: Once done, remove from the oven and let them cool slightly before serving. Remove toothpicks before eating.

# KETO COLESLAW

**Serving Size:** 6
Prep Time: 15 minutes
Cooking Time: 0 minutes

**Nutrition Info: (Per serving)**
- Calories: 120
- Total Fat: 10g
- Cholesterol: 10mg
- Sodium: 200mg
- Total Carbohydrates: 5g
- Dietary Fiber: 2g
- Sugars: 2g
- Protein: 2g

**Ingredients:**
- 1 small head of green cabbage, shredded
- 2 medium carrots, grated
- 1/2 cup mayonnaise

- 2 tablespoons apple cider vinegar
- 1 tablespoon Dijon mustard
- 1-2 tablespoons powdered erythritol or preferred keto-friendly sweetener
- Salt and pepper to taste
- Chopped fresh parsley or chives for garnish (optional)

**Directions**:
1. Prepare Vegetables: Start by shredding the cabbage and grating the carrots. Place them in a large mixing bowl.
2. Make Dressing: In a separate bowl, whisk together the mayonnaise, apple cider vinegar, Dijon mustard, powdered erythritol, salt, and pepper until well combined. Adjust the sweetness and seasoning according to your taste.
3. Combine Ingredients: Pour the dressing over the shredded cabbage and carrots. Toss everything together until the vegetables are evenly coated with the dressing.
4. Chill: Cover the bowl with plastic wrap or a lid and refrigerate the coleslaw for at least 1 hour before serving. This allows the flavors to meld together and for the cabbage to slightly soften.
5. Serve: Once chilled, give the coleslaw a final toss and garnish with chopped fresh parsley or chives if desired. Serve cold as a refreshing side dish with your favorite keto-friendly meals.

# CHAPTER 6
## IRRESISTIBLE SNACKS

## CHEESY GARLIC BREADSTICKS

**Serving Size**: 4-6
Prep Time: 15 minutes
Cooking Time: 20 minutes

**Nutrition Info: (Per serving)**
- Calories: 220
- Total Fat: 10g
- Cholesterol: 25mg
- Sodium: 480mg
- Total Carbohydrates: 25g
- Dietary Fiber: 1g
- Sugars: 2g
- Protein: 8g

**Ingredients:**
- 1 pound pizza dough (store-bought or homemade)
- 2 tablespoons butter, melted
- 2 cloves garlic, minced
- 1 cup shredded mozzarella cheese
- 1/4 cup grated Parmesan cheese
- 1 teaspoon dried oregano
- 1 teaspoon dried basil
- Salt and pepper to taste
- Marinara sauce (for dipping, optional)

**Directions:**

1. Preheat Oven: Preheat your oven to 425°F (220°C). Line a baking sheet with parchment paper or lightly grease it.
2. Prepare Dough: Roll out the pizza dough on a lightly floured surface into a rectangle about 1/4-inch thick. Transfer the dough to the prepared baking sheet.
3. Prepare Garlic Butter: In a small bowl, mix the melted butter and minced garlic. Brush this mixture evenly over the rolled-out dough.
4. Add Cheese and Seasonings: Sprinkle the shredded mozzarella cheese and grated Parmesan cheese evenly over the dough. Then, sprinkle the dried oregano, dried basil, salt, and pepper on top of the cheese.
5. Bake: Bake in the preheated oven for about 15-20 minutes, or until the edges are golden brown and the cheese is melted and bubbly.
6. Slice and Serve: Once done, remove from the oven and let cool for a few minutes. Use a pizza cutter or sharp knife to slice the cheesy bread into sticks. Serve warm with marinara sauce for dipping if desired.

# ZUCCHINI CHIPS

**Serving Size:** 4
Prep Time: 10 minutes
Cooking Time: 2 hours

**Nutrition Info: (Per serving)**
- Calories: 50
- Total Fat: 3g
- Cholesterol: 0mg
- Sodium: 150mg
- Total Carbohydrates: 6g
- Dietary Fiber: 1g

- Sugars: 2g
- Protein: 1g

**Ingredients**:
- 2 medium zucchinis
- 1 tablespoon olive oil
- 1 teaspoon sea salt
- 1/2 teaspoon black pepper
- Optional: 1/2 teaspoon garlic powder or paprika for extra flavor

**Directions**:
1. Preheat Oven: Preheat your oven to 225°F (110°C). Line two baking sheets with parchment paper or silicone baking mats.
2. Slice Zucchini: Using a mandoline slicer or a sharp knife, slice the zucchinis into thin, even rounds, about 1/8 inch thick.
3. Toss with Oil and Seasonings: In a large mixing bowl, toss the zucchini slices with olive oil until evenly coated. Sprinkle with sea salt, black pepper, and any optional seasonings you choose. Toss again to ensure all slices are seasoned.
4. Arrange on Baking Sheets: Arrange the zucchini slices in a single layer on the prepared baking sheets, making sure they do not overlap.
5. Bake: Place the baking sheets in the preheated oven. Bake for about 1.5 to 2 hours, or until the zucchini slices are crisp and golden brown. Check periodically to ensure they do not burn, rotating the baking sheets halfway through for even cooking.
6. Cool and Serve: Once the zucchini chips are crisp, remove them from the oven and let them cool on the baking sheets. They will continue to crisp up as they cool.

7. Store: If you have leftovers, store the cooled zucchini chips in an airtight container at room temperature for up to 3 days to maintain their crispiness.

# AVOCADO DEVILED EGGS

**Serving Size**: 6
Prep Time: 15 minutes
Cooking Time: 10 minutes

**Nutrition Info: (Per serving)**
- Calories: 120
- Total Fat: 10g
- Cholesterol: 165mg
- Sodium: 140mg
- Total Carbohydrates: 2g
- Dietary Fiber: 1g
- Sugars: 0g
- Protein: 6g

**Ingredients:**
- 6 large eggs
- 1 ripe avocado
- 1 tablespoon lime juice
- 1 tablespoon mayonnaise
- 1 teaspoon Dijon mustard
- 1 clove garlic, minced
- Salt and pepper to taste
- Paprika for garnish
- Chopped fresh cilantro or chives for garnish

**Directions:**
1. Boil Eggs: Place the eggs in a saucepan and cover them with cold water. Bring the water to a boil over

medium-high heat. Once boiling, remove from heat and cover the pan. Let the eggs sit in the hot water for 9-12 minutes, depending on your desired level of doneness.

2. Cool and Peel Eggs: Transfer the eggs to a bowl of ice water to cool completely. Once cooled, peel the eggs and slice them in half lengthwise.

3. Remove Yolks: Carefully remove the yolks and place them in a medium bowl. Set the egg whites aside on a serving platter.

4. Prepare Filling: In the bowl with the egg yolks, add the avocado, lime juice, mayonnaise, Dijon mustard, and minced garlic. Mash the mixture until smooth and creamy. Season with salt and pepper to taste.

5. Fill Egg Whites: Spoon or pipe the avocado mixture into the egg white halves, filling each cavity generously.

6. Garnish and Serve: Sprinkle a pinch of paprika over the filled eggs for a touch of color. Garnish with chopped fresh cilantro or chives if desired.

# PEPPERONI PIZZA BITES

**Serving Size:** 4
Prep Time: 15 minutes
Cooking Time: 15 minutes

**Nutrition Info: (Per serving)**
- Calories: 220
- Total Fat: 12g
- Cholesterol: 30mg
- Sodium: 600mg
- Total Carbohydrates: 20g
- Dietary Fiber: 1g
- Sugars: 3g
- Protein: 10g

**Ingredients:**
- 1 can (8 ounces) refrigerated crescent roll dough
- 24 slices of pepperoni
- 4 string cheese sticks, each cut into 6 pieces
- 1 cup marinara or pizza sauce for dipping
- 1 tablespoon melted butter
- 1 teaspoon garlic powder
- 1 teaspoon Italian seasoning
- Grated Parmesan cheese (optional)

**Directions:**
1. Preheat Oven: Preheat your oven to 375°F (190°C).
2. Prepare Dough: Open the can of crescent roll dough and unroll it. Separate it into 8 triangles as per the package instructions.
3. Assemble Bites: Cut each triangle in half to make 16 smaller triangles. Place a slice of pepperoni on each triangle, followed by a piece of string cheese.
4. Roll and Seal: Roll up each triangle, starting from the wider end and rolling towards the point. Pinch the seams to seal the dough around the filling.
5. Season and Bake: Place the rolled bites on a baking sheet lined with parchment paper. Brush the tops with melted butter and sprinkle with garlic powder, Italian seasoning, and grated Parmesan cheese if desired.
6. Bake: Bake in the preheated oven for 12-15 minutes, or until the bites are golden brown and the cheese is melted.
7. Serve: Remove from the oven and let cool for a few minutes. Serve warm with marinara or pizza sauce for dipping.

# SPICY ROASTED ALMONDS

**Serving Size**: 8
Prep Time: 10 minutes
Cooking Time: 20 minutes

**Nutrition Info: (Per serving)**
- Calories: 200
- Total Fat: 18g
- Cholesterol: 0mg
- Sodium: 150mg
- Total Carbohydrates: 7g
- Dietary Fiber: 4g
- Sugars: 2g
- Protein: 6g

**Ingredients**:
- 2 cups raw almonds
- 1 tablespoon olive oil
- 1 teaspoon smoked paprika
- 1/2 teaspoon cayenne pepper (adjust to taste)
- 1 teaspoon garlic powder
- 1 teaspoon onion powder
- 1 teaspoon salt
- 1/2 teaspoon black pepper
- 1 tablespoon honey (optional for a touch of sweetness)

**Directions**:
1. Preheat Oven: Preheat your oven to 350°F (175°C).
2. Prepare Almonds: In a large mixing bowl, combine the raw almonds with olive oil. Stir well to ensure the almonds are evenly coated.
3. Add Spices: Add the smoked paprika, cayenne pepper, garlic powder, onion powder, salt, and black pepper to the

bowl. If you prefer a hint of sweetness, add the honey as well. Mix everything thoroughly until the almonds are evenly coated with the spice mixture.

4. Arrange on Baking Sheet: Spread the spiced almonds in a single layer on a baking sheet lined with parchment paper.

5. Roast Almonds: Place the baking sheet in the preheated oven and roast for about 15-20 minutes, stirring halfway through to ensure even roasting. Keep a close eye on them towards the end to prevent burning.

6. Cool: Once the almonds are roasted to your desired level of crispiness, remove them from the oven and let them cool completely on the baking sheet. The almonds will become crunchier as they cool.

7. Serve: After cooling, transfer the spicy roasted almonds to a serving bowl or an airtight container for storage. They can be enjoyed as a healthy snack or added to salads for an extra crunch.

# CUCUMBER CREAM CHEESE BITES

**Serving Size:** 12 bites
Prep Time: 15 minutes
Cooking Time: None

**Nutrition Info: (Per serving)**
- Calories: 50
- Total Fat: 4g
- Cholesterol: 10mg
- Sodium: 70mg
- Total Carbohydrates: 2g
- Dietary Fiber: 0.5g

- Sugars: 1g
- Protein: 1g

## Ingredients:
- 1 large cucumber
- 4 ounces cream cheese, softened
- 1 tablespoon fresh dill, finely chopped
- 1 tablespoon fresh chives, finely chopped
- 1 teaspoon lemon juice
- Salt and pepper to taste
- Optional: smoked salmon slices or cherry tomato halves for garnish

## Directions:
1. Prepare Cucumber: Wash and dry the cucumber. Using a vegetable peeler, partially peel the cucumber to create alternating stripes of peeled and unpeeled sections. Slice the cucumber into 1/2-inch thick rounds.
2. Make Cream Cheese Mixture: In a medium bowl, combine the softened cream cheese, fresh dill, fresh chives, lemon juice, salt, and pepper. Mix until smooth and well combined.
3. Assemble Bites: Lay the cucumber slices flat on a serving platter. Using a small spoon or a piping bag with a star tip, dollop or pipe the cream cheese mixture onto each cucumber slice.
4. Optional Garnish: If desired, top each cucumber cream cheese bite with a small piece of smoked salmon or a cherry tomato half for added flavor and visual appeal.
5. Serve: Serve immediately or refrigerate until ready to serve. These bites are best enjoyed fresh but can be made a few hours in advance.

# CHAPTER 7 SWEET TREATS

## CHOCOLATE AVOCADO MOUSSE

**Serving Size**: 4
Prep Time: 10 minutes
Cooking Time: 0 minutes

**Nutrition Info: (Per serving)**
- Calories: 250
- Total Fat: 18g
- Cholesterol: 0mg
- Sodium: 20mg
- Total Carbohydrates: 24g
- Dietary Fiber: 7g
- Sugars: 14g
- Protein: 3g

**Ingredients:**
- 2 ripe avocados
- 1/4 cup unsweetened cocoa powder
- 1/4 cup maple syrup or honey
- 1/4 cup unsweetened almond milk (or any milk of choice)
- 1 teaspoon vanilla extract
- Pinch of salt
- Optional toppings: fresh berries, shaved chocolate, whipped cream

**Directions:**
1. Prepare Avocados: Cut the avocados in half, remove the pits, and scoop the flesh into a blender or food processor.
2. Blend Ingredients: Add the cocoa powder, maple syrup or honey, almond milk, vanilla extract, and a pinch of salt to the blender with the avocados.
3. Blend Until Smooth: Blend all the ingredients until the mixture is smooth and creamy. You may need to stop and scrape down the sides of the blender or food processor a couple of times to ensure everything is well combined.
4. Adjust Sweetness: Taste the mousse and adjust the sweetness or cocoa powder to your preference. If you like it sweeter, add a bit more maple syrup or honey.
5. Chill (Optional): For a firmer texture, you can chill the mousse in the refrigerator for about 30 minutes before serving.
6. Serve: Spoon the chocolate avocado mousse into serving dishes and top with optional toppings like fresh berries, shaved chocolate, or a dollop of whipped cream.

# ALMOND FLOUR CHOCOLATE CHIP COOKIES

**Serving Size**: 12 cookies
Prep Time: 10 minutes
Cooking Time: 15 minutes

**Nutrition Info: (Per cookie)**
- Calories: 150
- Total Fat: 11g
- Saturated Fat: 4g
- Cholesterol: 20mg

- Sodium: 100mg
- Total Carbohydrates: 10g
- Dietary Fiber: 2g
- Sugars: 7g
- Protein: 4g

**Ingredients:**
- 2 cups almond flour
- 1/2 teaspoon baking soda
- 1/4 teaspoon salt
- 1/4 cup coconut oil or unsalted butter, melted
- 1/4 cup maple syrup or honey
- 1 large egg
- 1 teaspoon vanilla extract
- 1/2 cup dark chocolate chips

**Directions:**
1. Preheat Oven: Preheat your oven to 350°F (175°C). Line a baking sheet with parchment paper.
2. Mix Dry Ingredients: In a medium bowl, whisk together the almond flour, baking soda, and salt.
3. Combine Wet Ingredients: In a separate large bowl, mix the melted coconut oil (or butter), maple syrup (or honey), egg, and vanilla extract until well combined.
4. Form Dough: Add the dry ingredients to the wet ingredients and mix until a dough forms. Stir in the chocolate chips.
5. Shape Cookies: Using a tablespoon or a small cookie scoop, drop the dough onto the prepared baking sheet, spacing the cookies about 2 inches apart. Flatten them slightly with your fingers or the back of a spoon.
6. Bake: Bake in the preheated oven for 12-15 minutes, or until the edges are golden brown.

7. Cool: Allow the cookies to cool on the baking sheet for 5 minutes before transferring them to a wire rack to cool completely.

# COCONUT FAT BOMBS

**Serving Size**: 12 fat bombs
Prep Time: 10 minutes
Cooking Time: 0 minutes (chill time: 30 minutes)

**Nutrition Info: (Per serving)**
- Calories: 110
- Total Fat: 11g
- Saturated Fat: 9g
- Cholesterol: 5mg
- Sodium: 10mg
- Total Carbohydrates: 2g
- Dietary Fiber: 1g
- Sugars: 1g
- Protein: 1g

**Ingredients:**
- 1/2 cup coconut oil
- 1/2 cup unsweetened shredded coconut
- 1/4 cup almond butter or peanut butter
- 2 tablespoons cocoa powder
- 1 tablespoon sweetener (like stevia, erythritol, or honey)
- 1 teaspoon vanilla extract
- Pinch of salt

Directions:
1. Melt Coconut Oil: In a small saucepan over low heat, melt the coconut oil until it's fully liquid. Alternatively, you

can microwave it in a microwave-safe bowl for about 30 seconds.

2. Mix Ingredients: In a medium mixing bowl, combine the melted coconut oil, unsweetened shredded coconut, almond butter, cocoa powder, sweetener, vanilla extract, and a pinch of salt. Stir until all ingredients are well combined and smooth.

3. Fill Molds: Pour the mixture into silicone molds or ice cube trays, filling each cavity about three-quarters full. You can use a spoon or a small measuring cup to help with this.

4. Chill: Place the molds in the refrigerator or freezer for about 30 minutes, or until the fat bombs are firm to the touch.

5. Store and Serve: Once set, remove the fat bombs from the molds. Store them in an airtight container in the refrigerator for up to two weeks or in the freezer for up to a month. Serve chilled.

# SUGAR-FREE CHEESECAKE BITES

**Serving Size**: 12 bites
Prep Time: 20 minutes
Cooking Time: 10 minutes (plus chilling time)

**Nutrition Info: (Per serving)**
- Calories: 110
- Total Fat: 9g
- Cholesterol: 30mg
- Sodium: 90mg
- Total Carbohydrates: 4g
- Dietary Fiber: 0g

- Sugars: 1g (from natural ingredients)
- Protein: 3g

**Ingredients:**
For the crust:
- 1 cup almond flour
- 2 tablespoons melted butter
- 2 tablespoons granulated sugar substitute (e.g., erythritol or stevia blend)
- 1/2 teaspoon cinnamon
For the filling:
- 8 ounces cream cheese, softened
- 1/4 cup granulated sugar substitute
- 1 teaspoon vanilla extract
- 1/4 cup heavy cream
- Fresh berries for topping (optional)

**Directions:**
1. Prepare Crust: In a medium bowl, combine the almond flour, melted butter, granulated sugar
substitute, and cinnamon. Mix until the mixture resembles wet sand.
2. Form Crust: Line a mini muffin tin with paper liners. Press about a tablespoon of the almond flour mixture into the bottom of each liner to form the crust. Use the back of a spoon to press it down firmly.
3. Bake Crust: Preheat your oven to 350°F (175°C). Bake the crusts for about 5-7 minutes, or until they are lightly golden. Remove from the oven and let them cool completely.
4. Prepare Filling: In a large mixing bowl, beat the softened cream cheese with an electric mixer until smooth. Add the granulated sugar substitute and vanilla extract, and continue to beat until well combined.

Gradually add the heavy cream and beat until the mixture is smooth and creamy.

5. Fill Cups: Once the crusts are cool, spoon the cream cheese mixture into each crust, filling them to the top. Smooth the tops with the back of a spoon or a small spatula.

6. Chill: Place the cheesecake bites in the refrigerator and chill for at least 2 hours, or until they are firm and set.

7. Serve: Before serving, top each cheesecake bite with fresh berries if desired. Serve chilled.

# LEMON POPPY SEED MUFFINS

**Serving Size**: 12 muffins
Prep Time: 15 minutes
Cooking Time: 20 minutes

**Nutrition Info: (Per muffin)**
- Calories: 180
- Total Fat: 8g
- Cholesterol: 30mg
- Sodium: 180mg
- Total Carbohydrates: 24g
- Dietary Fiber: 1g
- Sugars: 12g
- Protein: 3g

**Ingredients:**
- 2 cups all-purpose flour
- 1/2 cup granulated sugar
- 1/4 cup brown sugar
- 2 teaspoons baking powder
- 1/2 teaspoon baking soda
- 1/4 teaspoon salt

- Zest of 2 lemons
- 1/2 cup unsalted butter, melted and cooled
- 1/2 cup plain yogurt
- 1/4 cup fresh lemon juice
- 2 large eggs
- 1 teaspoon vanilla extract
- 2 tablespoons poppy seeds

**Directions:**
1. Preheat Oven: Preheat your oven to 375°F (190°C). Line a 12-cup muffin tin with paper liners or grease the cups with cooking spray.
2. Mix Dry Ingredients: In a large mixing bowl, whisk together the flour, granulated sugar, brown sugar, baking powder, baking soda, salt, and lemon zest until well combined.
3. Combine Wet Ingredients: In another bowl, whisk together the melted butter, yogurt, lemon juice, eggs, and vanilla extract until smooth.
4. Combine Mixtures: Pour the wet ingredients into the dry ingredients and stir until just combined. Do not overmix; a few lumps are okay. Fold in the poppy seeds.
5. Fill Muffin Cups: Divide the batter evenly among the prepared muffin cups, filling each about 2/3 full.
6. Bake: Place the muffin tin in the preheated oven and bake for about 18-20 minutes or until a toothpick inserted into the center of a muffin comes out clean.
7. Cool and Serve: Remove the muffins from the oven and let them cool in the tin for 5 minutes. Then transfer them to a wire rack to cool completely.
8. Optional Glaze: If desired, you can drizzle the cooled muffins with a simple glaze made of powdered sugar and lemon juice for extra sweetness and tanginess.

# CHAPTER 8 DRINKS AND BEVERAGES

## KETO ICED MATCHA LATTE

**Serving Size**: 1
Prep Time: 5 minutes
Cooking Time: 0 minutes

**Nutrition Info: (Per serving)**
- Calories: 120
- Total Fat: 10g
- Cholesterol: 0mg
- Sodium: 10mg
- Total Carbohydrates: 3g
- Dietary Fiber: 1g
- Sugars: 0g
- Protein: 2g

**Ingredients:**
- 1 teaspoon matcha powder
- 1 cup unsweetened almond milk (or any low-carb milk of your choice)
- 1 tablespoon MCT oil (optional, for added creaminess)
- Liquid stevia or your preferred keto-friendly sweetener to taste
- Ice cubes

**Directions**:
1. Prepare Matcha: In a glass, add the matcha powder and a small amount of hot water. Whiskvigorously until the matcha is fully dissolved and no clumps remain.
2. Add Sweetener: Sweeten the matcha to taste using liquid stevia or your preferred keto-friendly sweetener. Stir until well combined.
3. Mix with Milk: Add the unsweetened almond milk to the glass with the matcha mixture. If using MCT oil for added creaminess, add it to the glass as well. Stir everything together until well combined.
4. Add Ice: Fill the glass with ice cubes to make it an iced latte.
5. Serve: Stir the iced matcha latte once more before serving to ensure everything is evenly mixed and chilled.

# LOW CARB BERRY SMOOTHIE

**Serving Size**: 2
Prep Time: 5 minutes
Cooking Time: 0 minutes

**Nutrition Info: (Per serving)**
- Calories: 120
- Total Fat: 1g
- Cholesterol: 0mg
- Sodium: 10mg
- Total Carbohydrates: 15g
- Dietary Fiber: 5g
- Sugars: 7g
- Protein: 8g

**Ingredients:**
- 1 cup frozen mixed berries (such as strawberries, blueberries, and raspberries)
- 1 cup unsweetened almond milk (or any milk of your choice)
- 1/2 cup plain Greek yogurt
- 1 tablespoon chia seeds
- 1 tablespoon sugar-free sweetener (optional, adjust to taste)
- Ice cubes (optional, for a thicker smoothie)

**Directions:**
1. Gather Ingredients: Collect all the ingredients needed for the smoothie.
2. Blend: In a blender, combine the frozen mixed berries, almond milk, Greek yogurt, chia seeds, and sugar-free sweetener (if using). Blend until smooth and creamy. If you prefer a thicker smoothie, add a few ice cubes and blend again until desired consistency is reached.
3. Serve: Pour the low carb berry smoothie into glasses and garnish with fresh berries or a sprinkle of chia seeds if desired.
4. Enjoy: Serve immediately and enjoy your refreshing and nutritious low carb berry smoothie!

# KETO ELECTROLYTE LEMONADE

**Serving Size**: 2
Prep Time: 5 minutes
Cooking Time: 0 minutes

**Nutrition Info: (Per serving)**
- Calories: 10

- Total Fat: 0g
- Cholesterol: 0mg
- Sodium: 700mg
- Total Carbohydrates: 2g
- Dietary Fiber: 0g
- Sugars: 0g
- Protein: 0g

**Ingredients:**
- 2 cups water
- 1/2 teaspoon salt
- 1/4 teaspoon potassium chloride (optional)
- 1/4 teaspoon magnesium citrate powder (optional)
- 1 tablespoon fresh lemon juice
- 1-2 tablespoons erythritol or your preferred keto-friendly sweetener (adjust to taste)
- Ice cubes
- Lemon slices (for garnish, optional)
- Fresh mint leaves (for garnish, optional)

**Directions:**
1. Prepare Ingredients: Gather all the ingredients needed for the keto electrolyte lemonade.
2. Mix Electrolytes: In a pitcher, combine water, salt, potassium chloride (if using), and magnesium citrate powder (if using). Stir well until the salt and powders are completely dissolved.
3. Add Flavor: Add fresh lemon juice and erythritol (or your preferred sweetener) to the pitcher. Stir until the sweetener is dissolved and the lemonade is well mixed.
4. Chill and Serve: Add ice cubes to the pitcher or pour the lemonade over ice in individual glasses. Garnish with lemon slices and fresh mint leaves if desired.

5. Enjoy: Serve your refreshing keto electrolyte lemonade immediately. It's a perfect way to stay hydrated and replenish electrolytes while following a keto diet.

# LOW CARB MOCHA FRAPPÉ

**Serving Size**: 1
Prep Time: 5 minutes
Cooking Time: 0 minutes

**Nutrition Info: (Per serving)**
- Calories: 120
- Total Fat: 7g
- Cholesterol: 5mg
- Sodium: 80mg
- Total Carbohydrates: 6g
- Dietary Fiber: 2g
- Sugars: 1g
- Protein: 8g

**Ingredients:**
- 1 cup brewed coffee, chilled
- 1/2 cup unsweetened almond milk (or any milk of choice)
- 1 tablespoon cocoa powder
- 1 tablespoon erythritol (or sweetener of choice)
- 1/2 teaspoon vanilla extract
- 1 cup ice cubes
- Whipped cream (optional, for topping)
- Sugar-free chocolate syrup (optional, for drizzling)

**Directions:**
1. Brew Coffee: Brew a cup of coffee and let it cool completely. You can also use leftover chilled coffee.

2. Blend Ingredients: In a blender, combine the chilled brewed coffee, unsweetened almond milk, cocoa powder, erythritol, vanilla extract, and ice cubes.
3. Blend until Smooth: Blend everything until smooth and creamy. If the frappé is too thick, you can add a splash of almond milk or water to adjust the consistency.
4. Pour and Serve: Pour the mocha frappé into a tall glass. If desired, top it with whipped cream and drizzle with sugar-free chocolate syrup for an extra indulgent touch.
5. Enjoy: Insert a straw and enjoy your refreshing low-carb mocha frappé!

# KETO CUCUMBER MINT COOLER

**Serving Size:** 2
Prep Time: 10 minutes
Cooking Time: 0 minutes

**Nutrition Info: (Per serving)**
- Calories: 15
- Total Fat: 0g
- Cholesterol: 0mg
- Sodium: 5mg
- Total Carbohydrates: 3g
- Dietary Fiber: 1g
- Sugars: 1g
- Protein: 1g

**Ingredients:**
- 1 medium cucumber, peeled and chopped
- 10-12 fresh mint leaves
- 2 cups cold water
- 2 tablespoons fresh lime juice

- 1-2 tablespoons keto-friendly sweetener (like stevia or erythritol)
- Ice cubes
- Fresh mint sprigs for garnish
- Slices of lime for garnish

**Directions**:
1. Prepare Ingredients: Start by peeling and chopping the cucumber. Gather fresh mint leaves, lime juice, keto-friendly sweetener, and cold water.
2. Blend Ingredients: In a blender, combine the chopped cucumber, fresh mint leaves, lime juice, keto-friendly sweetener, and cold water. Blend until smooth.
3. Strain (optional): If you prefer a smoother consistency, you can strain the mixture using a fine
mesh sieve or cheesecloth to remove any pulp.
4. Chill: Transfer the cucumber mint mixture to a pitcher and refrigerate until chilled, about 1 hour.
5. Serve: Fill glasses with ice cubes. Pour the chilled cucumber mint mixture into the glasses. Garnish each glass with a sprig of fresh mint and a slice of lime.
6. Enjoy: Stir gently and enjoy your refreshing Keto Cucumber Mint Cooler!

# LOW CARB TURMERIC GOLDEN MILK

**Serving Size**: 1
Prep Time: 5 minutes
Cooking Time: 10 minutes
Nutrition Info: (Per serving)
- Calories: 120
- Total Fat: 7g

- Cholesterol: 0mg
- Sodium: 30mg
- Total Carbohydrates: 6g
- Dietary Fiber: 1g
- Sugars: 3g
- Protein: 4g

**Ingredients:**
- 1 cup unsweetened almond milk
- 1/2 teaspoon ground turmeric
- 1/4 teaspoon ground cinnamon
- 1/4 teaspoon ground ginger
- 1 pinch ground black pepper
- 1 teaspoon coconut oil or ghee
- 1 teaspoon low-carb sweetener (like stevia or erythritol), optional
- 1/2 teaspoon vanilla extract, optional

**Directions:**
1. Heat Milk: In a small saucepan, heat the almond milk over medium-low heat until it's warm but not boiling.
2. Mix Ingredients: Add the ground turmeric, cinnamon, ginger, black pepper, coconut oil or ghee, low-carb sweetener (if using), and vanilla extract (if using) to the warm almond milk. Whisk everything together until well combined.
3. Simmer: Let the mixture simmer gently for about 5-7 minutes, stirring occasionally. This helps to infuse the flavors and dissolve the spices.
4. Strain and Serve: After simmering, strain the golden milk through a fine mesh sieve or cheesecloth to remove any remaining spice particles. Pour the strained golden milk into a mug.

5. Enjoy: Your low-carb turmeric golden milk is ready to be enjoyed! You can sprinkle a little extra cinnamon on top for garnish if desired.

# CONCLUSION

Congratulations on completing the **Easy and Quick Ketogenic Cookbook**!

You've taken a significant step towards embracing a healthier lifestyle, and we hope this journey has been as rewarding and enjoyable for you as it has been for us to share it with you. The ketogenic diet offers a multitude of benefits, from improved energy levels and mental clarity to sustainable weight management and overall wellness. But more than that, it provides a way to reconnect with the joys of cooking and eating delicious, wholesome food.

As you've discovered, eating keto doesn't have to mean spending hours in the kitchen or struggling with complicated recipes. The meals in this cookbook are designed to be simple, quick, and full of flavor, making it easy to stick to your health goals without feeling deprived or overwhelmed.

Here are a few final tips to help you continue your keto journey with confidence:

1. **Plan Ahead:** Keep your pantry stocked with keto-friendly staples and plan your meals for the week. This will save you time and ensure you always have ingredients on hand for quick, healthy meals.
2. **Experiment and Customize:** Don't be afraid to get creative with the recipes. Adjust flavors and

ingredients to suit your taste preferences and dietary needs. The keto diet is flexible and can be tailored to fit your lifestyle.

3. **Stay Hydrated and Mindful of Electrolytes:** Drinking plenty of water and maintaining your electrolyte balance is crucial on the keto diet. Incorporate foods rich in potassium, magnesium, and sodium to keep your body functioning optimally.

4. **Enjoy the Journey:** Remember that eating well is about more than just the food. It's about enjoying the process, sharing meals with loved ones, and taking pride in nourishing your body.

I hope this cookbook has provided you with not only recipes but also inspiration and confidence to continue exploring the wonderful world of ketogenic cooking. Each dish is a step towards better health, and every meal is an opportunity to savor the flavors and benefits of the keto lifestyle.

Thank you for allowing me to be part of your culinary adventure. I wish you all the best on your path to health and happiness. Keep cooking, keep experimenting, and most importantly, keep enjoying every bite.

Bon appétit!

Mary M. Vanish

Made in the USA
Middletown, DE
22 July 2024

57802160R00056